SLEEPERS OF BEULAH

SLEEPERS
OF BEULAH

GABRIEL LEVIN

SINCLAIR-STEVENSON

First published in Great Britain by
Sinclair-Stevenson Limited
7/8 Kendrick Mews
London SW7 3HG England

British Library Cataloguing in Publication Data
A CIP catalogue record for this book is available from the British Library.

ISBN: 1 85619 170 2 (hardback)
ISBN: 1 85619 196 6 (paperback)

Typeset by Rowland Phototypesetting Limited,
Bury St Edmunds, Suffolk

Printed and bound in Great Britain by
Clays Limited, St Ives plc

For Anat

ACKNOWLEDGMENTS

Some of the poems in this collection originally appeared in *Ariel*, *The Literary Review*, *London Magazine*, *Poets Cornered: The Jerusalem Post*, *Poet Lore*, *Shirim*, *Southwest Review*, and *Tikkun*.

CONTENTS

The pilgrims fly because they plod.

Empson

A TARDY QASIDA

Waking drenched in dew that honeycombs
and weakens the structure of rock –
are we as late as we seem, pitched
and feathered in the promise of the hour?
Picking our way through a crazyquilt
of ephemerals, dry stream beds braided
with heaps of gravel. To the east
mountains flounder in alluvial debris
(flash floods, writes al-Qais,
sending the ibexes hurtling down slopes).
A Boeing rumbles overhead
like a tectonic upheaval. There must be
something better to do than this,
stepping into the clearing
at the foot of the ore-bearing hills
where the copper-hungry once came.

Goat dung like peppercorns scattered
on the rough terrain where roaming
Midianites junked in the panic-grass
the white, sandstone face of Hathor (Lady
of Turquoise) with the chipped nose
and charcoal eyes. The cow-eared goddess
returns your gaze. Do you recognize
the look? Translate yourself, if you can,
into what is chiseled and reticently
conveyed in the smile: *sit down* (under
the spiny acacia) *stand up, place
yourself in the wind's path like a guide
who is well prepared*. One last desert
specimen plucked and dropped in the satchel,
the Citroën idle at the ravine's mouth:
time to pick up and go, as the noonday sun
sinks its wellropes into the parched body.

You turn the ignition on and shift gears
on the pitted, dirt road. A pair
of bar-tailed, ground-dwelling desert larks
dart into the shrubs. Hadn't they been
trilling their exquisite, little heads off
a moment before being startled into flight?
The shimmering blacktop winds through
the temperate, central highlands. There are
floodplains here, traces of spillways
and drop structures channeling the runoff
water into the hillside cisterns.
The engine races north on ostrich legs –
can you believe it – lapping up miles
on a chassis of nuts and bolts, as a genesis
of odd, little words and rhythms
bubbles up to advertise the self
that would seize the ground of its being.

MEDITERRANEAN

Murex shells – the royal dye long squeezed
out of the hypobronchial gland – litter
the shore, where Sea People once heaved
long ships into the eastern basin, seeking her
who'd given them the slip: *Beauty*
they hallooed in her wake, or some such name
barked from the belly at the crass mutiny.
In their polychrome robes they stood in vain
gaping at the sea, the surf's short-
breathed plosives detonating in their ears.
Now I skin the busy beach for sport,
Lady-of-the-Sea, forever in arrears
of love, ears cocked to the pulmonary beat
of young hearts primed by the heat.

TURQUERIES

Curving east from the old Turkish railway
station, the road offers a sudden view
of the desert. I stare down the pinhead edge.
If there were only some way of speaking
of the whole ta-ta-boom beyond Dung Gate.
Sweetmeats, and the companionable *hookah*
to dream by. In Sultan's Pool the winter
sun pleases the backs of some tough cats.

I built a fire in Solomon's Stables
to warm my frostbitten poems. They'd been out
all night, walking the battlement walls
and calling under their breath, 'Suleiman,
Suleiman the Magnificent.' The flames
leaped and snorted like horses. Exhausted,
I flopped on the divan, determined to
cap my diwan with lines to the Sublime Porte.

The rosy Sultana showing her legs
is Mademoiselle de Clermont. A black page
lovingly fingers her pearls. The heart
flutters like a pigeon in the gutter
clotted with pine needles. I shall make
a grand entry into the city of God
and sob like a Frank, stumbling on the gold
leaf onion domes built by the Czar.

SONGS OF INNOCENCE

1

My watch, black-banded, with a scratch
      or two on its glassy-
eyed face, grips my wrist like a Roman
      handshake. Puzzled

by such doglike devotion, I listen to its
      stubborn subtraction,
knowing how in time hands will tire:
      the gazelle won't rise

2

from its haunches. Half my age, desirable,
      sprawled on pink
towels – immobile, eyes shut, dazed by fresh
      salvos of sun;

the sweet mosquito drone of the boy's motor-
      bikes invades
the shoreline: *move over old man.* I cut
      my losses,

3

and seal the cracks of my father's summer
      shack, now mine.
Sometimes I wear his bleached, straw hat.
      He took his death

unkindly; I watched over his grizzled
breath. No one here
now, but this quiet conspiracy, this
'Breathing together.'

ORANGES

'Oh, don't muss up my hair,' she said, as water lapped at her breasts and he gawked at it all: her floral patterned gown discarded on the pier, a wicker-basket brimming with fruit, and further along the shore, four nymphets doodling in the hot sand. Now's his chance.

March 1st. Alone in the garden, I imagine workable endings to the tale. Elopement. The baffled family in Tyre? 'One must be absolutely modern' (Rimbaud, before sailing to Aden). I think I'll sit here with coffee and book. Europa? Entangled in his arms. Orange rinds on the floor.

THREE SORTIES OUT OF THE CITY WALLS

(Melville, 1857)

1. Lion's Gate

Glutted summer where the dove homes
over the tombs, addresses the wound
whitening the seasonless land
(here some lie).

The hillside taxed by our hands.
Lady of Recovery, pitted
by our frailty, your quiet pool
shadows my steps.

2. Kidron Valley

News from home is distant
and rare, backgammon days
with none to hear our praise.
Down the winding lane
the ghostliness of names,
along the stone-cut
troughs of our sphere,
Jehoshaphat at eventide;
with no grace of decay
and nowhere to hide,
night tapped the fool
on his way: I stepped aside.

3. Siloah's Pool

The basin is cold where I wash my face.
Season of indifferent rule, here
where the country mule
consoles the poor, nurses
the land's scraped vertebrae.

Is this the deity's embrace?
Where cats curl out of ruinous domes
and boys will sell our Lord
on a stick, deprived
of the sea's enormity of feeling.

(Mother of Solitude, feed my brain)

MOTHER GOOSE IN THE DESERT

Oh lord, let it rain
wet my little dress
that corn be cheaper
to fill my tummy

*

Oh rain, pour down
and let the geese
swim,

my little
niece is scab-headed

*

The wolf has caught
her, and gone to eating
he's gnawed her
to shreds in the ditch

ALL THE DAYS OF ADAM'S LIFE

Here is the little clearing
where I'd sit and gaze
into paradise, and here the spy-glass
through which I spied
on myself, so many smouldering

afternoons. Now I tamp
each name back into my foliate
brain, and close my lids
on the small, vanquished letters.

AMONG THE SCYTHIANS

'Lying on the wildgrass with a soft sadness
which is almost that of a woman,' the exiled
poet who taught the Art of Love and seemed a child
to Roman eyes, cannot shake off the madness
of his predicament: to be banished by Augustus
for having jauntily penned scenes of mild
abandon? Imagine having one's life-work filed
under the heading, Libidinous. *Tristesse*
knits his brows. Eyes drink in now the chilled
air and rustic colors (sky-in-rose-tatters)
of a new world that would abruptly derange
the senses: first fruits, mare's milk swilled
in a bowl, huntsmen in curious gear. It matters
we understand how all suffers change.

TARSHISH

Bramble tongue, not really but nearly.
All said and done you're just so far
from what we utter in an ordinary way:

crimp-breathed bird shaking its feathers
outside my window, with nothing
but evening shadows under its wings.

Rain-lashed tongue. The last eviction notice
snagged in the tree, the grand tableau
peeling viridian in the sun.

I have been getting it wrong a good part
of the day, meaning to speak along the ledge
where the cowl-hooded sparrows

stun the air. Must the slow evacuation
now begin, propped here among the evening software?
A sapling against your rude spine.

INNOCENTS ABROAD

Starting off in a downpour due east,
from under the portal the family
waves at the diminishing figures
in the collateral landscape of mind.
The small bell on the chrome bar
strangely urged us forward,
a stammer under the screwcap dome.
The Europe we'd hope to cover
'inch by inch' is pitched into the crisp
linguistic air. Again I read
of the sad passions obscuring our lives,
while the soberly dressed bulbul
sings secure in its weedtree pulpit,
pruned almost to perfection.
And in the empty house the inadequate
knowledge of our previous selves
is all that's left to wrap myself up in.
But we breakfast in the copious
fraction. The luminous centipede
uncurls its body, its feelers sweeping
down the wall. Dumbly articulate,
shuffling along on its sleeveless errand.

Clouds banked over the river,
a couloir of words leading nowhere,
or else up the steep embankment
of the imagination, to where Concord's
painted figure holds a large
carpenter's plane on her knees.
When I rub my eyes with my thumb
and forefinger nothing happens.
Lorenzetti's seated bather,
feet dangling in the water, won't break
the silence imposed like a curfew

on the promontory. Myriad the thoughts
concealed in the mind of the bather,
his back turned to a town 'bristling
with towers and tight within its walls.'
Looking back now, each day flung
like a quoit further out of reach.
Smile at the brave conception that brought us here.
Dream-embosked city. Ascending
streets, called ropeways, fruit-trees
trellised like a Byzantine meander
the length of the rough, stone walls.
This is the codex of rememberance
and its scholia (falteringly read
like a day-by-day primer).

Rummaging through my desk drawer.
Zephyr pencils, check stubs, cancelled
passports, an old draft of a poem
from Greece that makes me flinch.
Falling asleep in a field
of ruined columns. Delphi undoubtedly.
The guard shook my shoulder and spoke
in German, Nicht Shlaffen! Memory
holds the components apart,
like an exploded view. 'Don't leave,'
I call out to the figures
straying in the field.
Innocents abroad. The beau and the belle,
fading from view. 'At least,'
I whisper all to myself, 'drop me a line.'

The tungsten in the bulb casts its rude
light on the page. I can hear the rustle
of pigeons bedding down for the night
under the petticoat shag of the palm tree.
Jerusalem. 'Knobby,' writes Twain,
'with countless little domes

as a prison door is with bolt heads.'
December 9. The metaphor holds,
grimly. My daughter scrambles up
my knees to listen to another chapter
in *The Golden Geography*. Tonight
it's How the Earth's Surface Changes.
Some parts are sinking, others
slowly rising. She nods. Eyes glued,
however, to where words break off
and a biplane is led by the nose round
a smoking, pot-bellied volcano.

Remember the man behind the majestic
bellowphone, playing into the night,
the pedestrians drawn into a widening circle?
I thought I'd heard a phantasm of sounds,
it was as if an awkward new angel, with knowing eyes
and wings pinned to the driving,
easterly wind, flashed over the city,
broadcasting the inconsolable sum
of the ephemeral. And when the sounds
died, the crowd dispersed, reluctantly,
dragging their heels homeward,
singly, or in small, loose
bands. We walked up King George,
the bellowphonist's gold-lettered card
pressed in my wallet: L. H. SOLOMON,
MUSICIAN (WINDBAG), JUGGLER, MAGICIAN,
AT YOUR SERVICE. Perhaps the imagination
comes to this, dwelling elsewhere,
restive in its dispensations.
Stray gifts. The ever-delayed promise
of language before which we stand
amazed, so that even now I swivel round
to see who has taken the floor.

Consider for a moment any idea in its transitive
verbal form, and not a 'dumb picture
on a tablet.' The adequate idea, for instance,
of who we are, articulated within
the generous matrix of language. So I conceived
of it earlier in the day,
reading *The Ethics*. Do we become
what we are solely in the lines
unravelling before us?
The expression on your face
is varied and difficult to read, like a landscape –
say the cleft face of the city –
seen through a window and brushed
on canvas with quick-drying distemper.
From the old Gazelle Fort,
peering down: bullocked into the pit,
Moloch's burning wadi, its blackletter reality
still with us. You will stick around,
won't you? As yet another year is rung in
with a flurry of sirens and bells.

AN ARABIAN TALE

The installers arrive and extract precious instruments from their kit bags. One taps the walls with his topheavy wrench while his partner entangles himself in the rungs of the ladder like a clef. A third member of the party clucks his tongue with such delight on hearing the spigot thirst for water. – Who's left? Majnun, the layabout, whose heart is lashed to the beeper's song. Listen, as he listens-in to missed appointments, or those just made and somewhere jotted down by Answering Service girls. Lovely are the tidy messages fired from their lips into the motorola pinned to his brave overalls.

THE FERTILE CRESCENT

Jahiz of the bulging eyes claimed women
  beautiful whose torsos were stemlike
and buttocks a sand-dune. Each morning

dreaming up disquisitions on the apparent

transparency of the soul. Choose for yourself
  a simple, no nonsense style: sandalwood
rubbed too hard becomes hot, even noxious.

When the heart overheats – writes Saadia – the air

we draw into our lungs cools the vital
  organ (like blowing away excessive smoke
from a fire). Head-down, at a run,

you're ink from a quill, while a raillery
  of birdsong snips at your ears.
The wind in Baghdad sweeps the slate clean.

LETTER FROM OUTREMER

Tonight, arms folded in the Good
    Book, I dream a myriad
of sons and their restlessness.
    A friend has died.

Dust on the scales. I think of you,
    and the vast desert
frontier we roam, counting from
    the brow of each

small hill our gains and losses.
    Belligerence
on the high roads – the pack mules

are loaded with more than faith.
    A friend falls
from a rockface, and returns

in my restive sleep to mock
    our enterprise
with the last token of a smile.

PERSIAN MINIATURE

The king grew fonder by the hour of his silver coffer – and every night, the turban on his bulky head unwound, he would slip stealthily out of sight to examine what it might possibly offer. His wife, anxious to wish him goodnight, was obliged to shout into the empty halls he had long fled. Many songs were composed on this rich theme for our very beautiful, beautiful queen.

ALEPH

You'd think some
one had raised
the velvet hem

of the curtain,
had gazed and seen
the peaceable kingdom.

You'd think some
warm-blooded thing
had stepped out

of doors, had looked
at the moist face
of the earth, to cry

'Love, loosed
in the opening
seed!' But no.

Always the quiet
retreat. The forgetting.
Words, at a loss.

Clothes peeled
off the inflammable
body and heaped

on the cold, stone floor.

The unconcealed
earth, in the first
clearing of rain.

BOMBERG IN PALESTINE

She left him by the crushing machine
and gouged earth, while he set out
to recover the urgent forms: men shouldering
timber, shiftless in their bleak
surroundings. Light raking the wound.

THE CONFERENCE OF THE BIRDS

Simurgh. Sovereign bird whose loosed Persian feather tickles the nostrils of the inquisitive. Attar's book lies on the bed. My pencil marks the page where the dog of desire tugs at the fakir's heart. 'Renounce, renounce, renounce!' the cinnamon-colored Hoopoe cries to all the assembled birds. (We hear it as a clipped 'Hoo-hoo-hoo!'). But I swear we are all one happy family. No?

Earlier in the day I got a good look at a blackbird and heard it sing high up in the pines. A loud, ripping sound, and a high-pitched anxiety note, 'Tsee!' Did you know the blackbird will tilt its head to one side, listening for the earthworm as it tunnels through the subsoil? The Hoopoe, Solomon's keenest counsellor, clears its throat and prepares to reply.

OTHER SEAS

The Children's Crusade

They lit small, lively fires
across the sloping dunes and were quick
to act, their eyes darting here and there.
Bivouacked for the night, they now struck camp;
(we, dreaming of nothing, slept).
Blue-black embers crackled in the sand
long after the last boy folded his belongings.
Two pilgrims picked up in Italy remained;
an oversight . . . as were the water-skins
left to cool in the Mediterranean.

THE WILDERNESS OF JUDAEA

Ibex

I see it at noon:
clambering up the oblique
courses – the rough
escarpment; then turning

its wedge-shaped
muzzle: moist eyes taking
in the curious
flushed face of man.

Rock-Badger

We meet by a clump
of reeds. Shulamite's
spring not far off.
Aren't we a sight.

You – with your scuffle,
and pink, clipped
ears. Me – seeking a temporary
home among rocks.

THE ROAD TO JERUSALEM

Enquer me membra d'un mati
que nos fesem de guerra fi
    Guillaume IX of Aquitaine

Land that wolfs its inhabitants.
Remember the morning we lay down
our arms, love?
           The dog-eared leaves
in my Good Book speak of mandrakes in the field,

capers in the crevices. A portion
of my life drawing to an end – so I pictured
it in my mind, that toy, that bauble

where I idle away a good many hours –

looms close, yet vague, as a landmass
glimpsed from the sea – circumscribed,
suspect,
      like a lean, half-familiar
figure falling into stride beside me,
then lagging behind –
              'Who's there?'

I call out, wheeling round at my words.

SLEEPERS OF BEULAH

Suppose the city had swept
its dragnet across the rough grounds
of our lives. Dry runnels criss-
crossing the wadis peppered with low
lying shrubs called thorny burnet.
We who had dragged our feet, and slept
to the sound of the silver castanets
in the poplars, suddenly awoke
and gasped, as though sleep hadn't
drilled us properly to forget.
What was it now that shook us so?
Caterwauls, rising from under cover
of the wild mulberry tree,
or else human cries we had not imagined
possible. City quarried in stone
and hewed to the line. Even the bulbuls'
uncommon gossip in the foliage
appeared to press us on, unrelentingly.
Scampering down the Hill of Evil
Counsel, scrap-iron along the roadside.
We spoke in low, cautious tones;
the city would never lift its siege.

TABOR

Where a net is spread and the March oak,
wrapped in a light-green cloud, vaunts
its tenancy.
        Sometimes we fall into the fire,
sometimes into the water.
                But today
the mountain raises for orisons its dew
soaked dome:
        pronged vowels shepherding us
into the barley and mustard fields.

AEGYPT

Cartouche

Spun out of remote, unintelligible hands
the gift of the Nile. I am ferried
across the river and walk through
sugercane fields. A falcon with black-
tipped wings circles above the thorn
trees. In Menna's tomb his daughter
bends over the side of a morning-
barque to pluck a lotus leaf
from the river. Menna.
'Scribe of the fields of the lands.'

Rimbaud in Luxor

The horse-carts wake me up early. I lie
in bed scratching my balls; a dozen
hard strokes along the cleft and then,
as the itch starts to burn, I cup
my scrotum in my hands and caress
the skin with its sticky little hairs.
I am not myself. Riding up from
the Nubian desert, my skull indurating
in the sun, I could feel my white
skin being shucked off like candy-
wrapper. In the temple of the Ithyphallic
god *Min*, high up in the hypostyle,
facing the Nile, next to an erect phallus
and dwarfed bull on a leash, I cut
my name deep into the limestone.
And at dusk, as the fellahin – puzzled

by my looks – crowd around me, I watch
from my last home the sun embark
on its boat of a million years.

Nubia

It happens this way. Eyes peeled
on the Ibis scribbling its own hieratic
script in water. Elephantine Island –

of the Fish Eaters who journeyed into
Ethiopia with myrrh in their satchels
to spy out the land for Cambyses.

Dust clouds swirl above the granite
boulders jutting out of the wide river.
A boatman offers to take me down

the Nile to the stone face of the Angry
Man. I use the little words I have
to explain how I am fine here

in the shade of feluccas shored up
for caulking or a fresh coat of paint;
turning over in my mind the silent

stone processionals: cupbearers
and demonheads crowding the high walls,
funerary barques laden with offerings.

While all around me the crickets continue
their Song of Intervals — well on
into the morning, in the scorched grass.

Scarab

Dung grubber. Morning bug. *Ah'lan* little sun
creature of many forms. You creep up the rim
of my slouch hat left in the sand. Path
finder, I would take you back with me
to the land across the Great Bitter Lakes.

Cairo

for Keith Douglas 1920–44

Under the yellow light at Groppi's
tearoom, I think of you. Inhaling
the souk's sinister odours. Aniseed
on your breath, the garbled voices
. . . Nightfall powders the unfamiliar
streets with the scent of down-at-heel
angels; your 'Dishevelled ghosts,'
criss-crossing the trodden air.

Uneasy friend, caught in the ghostly
cadence of war, our strangeness tags
behind us like a faithful sandal-bearer. Days –
days, days and their ruthless light
over the unyielding city.
The large windows silver, giving
off a warm glow. I have wanted
to speak well of you.

Achmed Rassim

Francophone, one-time governor of Suez –
though fond of calling himself 'The poor
functionary' – poet of amorous weavings:
'Agostino Sinadino would like to know
what mythological path leads to the corolla
that stares at him with the cruel eyes
of a wounded horse.'
                    Iskandariya (stretch
the penultimate syllable, as the Arabs do);
battered, yellow-hooded, black-roofed cabs
drone like bees in the dusty warrens.
   Only yesterday, at dusk, sitting in your room
overlooking the tawny seafront, you jot
down the following: Madame Menamejjan –

devoted to his memory, alert – is amused
by my quest, but dismissive when it comes
to tracing his poems: 'My dear, I'm afraid
Rassim is lost to this world;' we meet
in a large hall, ringed with Angelo and Van Leo
studio portraits: Mirvat Amin, dolled up
and charming the camera; dreamy Iliana;
prim Ragaa Yousef; Samia in oriental dress;
Laila Taher, insouciant and darkly beautiful.

And at daybreak the rails wince and spark
under the first tram out – jolting you
awake. Open the shutters: neon Orange
Crush, Zagloul in cast-iron strides toward the sea;
street vendors, deaf to your pleas,
shout under the watchful Eye of Fatima.

This is why you have come to Alexandria.

The Desert Fathers

Driven out of their skins by solitude,
heaven vigilant as an electronic eye
and that newfangled word *eternity* kicking
like a stray bitch rings of dust
round their heels. And a certain old man
said, 'If you see a young novice
ascending by his own will up to heaven
catch him by the foot and throw him down.'

Throw him down to earth, where the rare
desert flora are scattered – milk vetch,
hairy saltworth and white wormwood;
where the keen-sighted lynx leaves its spoor
and the burrowing skink (who 'swims'
through loose sand) deposits its eggs.

Reading Dioscorus of Aphrodito

I think of the dimly-lit Ali Baba
where Mabruch the Monophysite
drowns his thirst with a *Stella*, one flight up,
windows open
over Midan Tahrir in May.
On top of Cairo's tallest building
Re, dolled up with one thousand
shuddering bulbs, sports a toupee. FLY
AIR EGYPT. I finger my doll
size cup of Turkish coffee, while Mabruch,
stiff in his chair, unglues
gloomy, lost-in-the-shuffle Coptic eyes
from the teeming square
and fixes his gaze on the rickety

table between us.
'May you ever steer the ship of state aright,
the beautiful, unshakeable eparchy.'

The Materials

El-Faiyum

for Dennis Silk

For a start the thick red smear of lips
prepared from mineral earths. He'd balked
at the idea of having his face chalked
up on a thin panel of cypress wood – bits
of finely ground carbon would do for the fixed
look in the eyes; the enlarged, shocked
pupils yielding to the emerging boxed-
in figure, his look-alike – and always had mixed
feelings when it came to art. Or rather,
to this funerary business: life summed up
in congealing wax, a few quick and well
applied strokes of the brush. Why bother?
Heavy shading on a chin that seems to jut
out from the cartonnage. 'Artemidorus, Farewell.'

PELICAN IN THE WILDERNESS

1

Summer at hand, and the golden
henbane shrivels in the lime-
stone wall, its root system exhausting
moisture absorbed into cement,
bits of soil collecting in chinks
where the gecko peers out, its eyes

protected by a watchglass covering
a moist, inner eyelid. The *Guide*
(Maimonides): to approach, touch, come near;
the abrupt entry – or union of thought
with what is observed (desired).
Orange speckled lichen feed on stone.

2

By June large tufts of bristles,
called pappus, top the roadside
milky thistle.
                    The hairy little
parachute is borne from the dried
flowerhead on the hot, Levant
wind.
            Each year the winter rains
wash away the red earth (terra
rossa) from the slopes.
                            The soil
erodes, leaving a scree of rubble.
A single dream coursing through
our lives, turns – imperceptibly –
into a mild, white fever.

3

How imagine the mind's essence,
dreamwork, rent from the gray
matter of the living body?

Peering into the yard, diurnal
net-winged midges –
no-see-ums – scale the steep

grade of air, in the cool of day.

Aleppo pine, cypress, the shadowing
pomegranate over the cistern.
Earth from which looms the house.

Starlings in the pinetops, then
out again, wings flapping. Not
conspicuous form but the virtue,

the notion through which a thing
becomes what it is. Perplexed,
leafing through your book at dusk –

a pelican in the wilderness.

4

A lone September pipistrelle
in the half-light, overhead.
Wing-swirl. Wrinkled, dried
pulp of the fig, underfoot.
                    Each day swiftly
draws to an end. (You stop

for breath.) Bone-meal raked
over the crust of earth,

waiting for the first rain.

Each day another page of small
print in the *Guide*. Apples of gold
in settings – eyelets – of silver,
words fitly spoken. Just poking
around, eyes for everything.

5

The huge carob tree coated in dust
   on the outskirts of Bethlehem.
A man in white keffiyeh vanishes
   under its shag to take a leak.
I've come to look at the straight
   flowering stalks of the squill
loosely scattered on the parched slopes.

   Fibrous, mute portenders
of Sweet Plum Rain. Rootstalks secure
   in their subterranean world.
To search out the maritime squill
   in a matrix of words, *Urginea
Maritima*. Its sap, digitalis-like
   i.e. a stimulant to the heart.

6

Birds. Fowl of the air. Here's one
draggling its tail-feather
in a puddle. Okay. Most of the time
I hear their ruckus up
in the sky, or on some rooftop
or sagging telegraph wire.
                        But you
and I, weren't we living on air,
planting our heels in the heart-
land's shifting sands? And it was
lovely, summer poking fun
at winter's poker face. Look at us
now – in quizzical November, I
offer you these lines: 'Gold, a beautiful
evil the ants (reared?) for man . . .'

Rag-tag December.
You'd like friends
to remember. Feeding
the wood-burner
dry sticks. It rained
so hard, scouring
the yard for kindling,
you settled for
the weekend paper.
What have you to lose?
The news, bold-faced,
burns in the grate.

Trip-wire days, who
grills the mirror

where the ghostly
anatomy won't answer,
or confess to its ashes?
Hapless boy, the storm-
windows will rattle
their jeopardy song:
narrow Jordan nobody's
crossing – each with
his gift from the cold
riverbed sings.

8

What is it you leave
    on the hard bed
of mid-winter? Warmth
    and light asleep.
Tired of this bone-
    house of yours, dear
Anima, your surest
    companion, leads you

by the hand, into
    the stubble field,
looking for the little
    speedwell they say
blossoms in January.

    Will you speak
of plenitude in the dead
    of winter? Admissions.
Retractions. Is that
    you? Picking up
the pieces – gingerly.

Fresh clumps of twisted needlegrass.
Spittle on the glume. *Diable*.
The Poor Man's Weatherglass paints
itself blue when the clouds part.

Let the spitballs fly in uncertain
March. Ankle deep in brick-red
vetchling. Storksbill. Shepherd's
purse ('What's that?' you ask,

pointing to the tiny, cordate pods).
Ramping fumitory. Pollen coughed
up in goodwill where the pine leans

over the lepers wall. So many names
indicative of simple existence –
the *Guide* again – and nothing else.

10

Where the sticky
fig buds in the pocket
of the wadi, rich in alluvial
silt. East of the watershed.
Imagine the slow burning
pith in the hollow fennel-stalk.
Fire cupped in the hand.
Part III, Prop. VI: is love –
amor – pleasure accompanied
by the idea of an external
cause? Potter's Field. Dwarf
shrubs stunted by goats

nibbling at young shoots.
Silwan, shimmering in the first
heat of the year. Brushfire
smoke in the eyes.

11

Slender wands of it rise from the ridge
   as you clamber up the footpath
   slipping. Teased by the lazy
braying of an ass. Traces of garden terraces.
   Puny, 'dusted' insects, having
   rifled the pollen sacs, check
out the hollyhock and seven-branched sage.
   The circle almost circled. And:

a narrative of day-time events offers
   a gentle, downward slope. I'm
   on tenterhooks, kicking off
fusty winter shoes by the swimming-hole.
   It's touch & go (hey little
   fruit fly – *shoo* now) here
in Baedeker's 'Wilderness.' The heart's
   an equivocal term. Dumb bird.

12

What shall we do with 'these hard,
dry and rather brittle views?'
Plein-air earth tones, a dour rockface
singularly
dazzled with noon light.

The brush laden with white impasto.
What then of the shifting
pockets of space – a topography of dips
and swells – between ciphers
that coax us like splotches of red,
into the fray?

                    It all spirals
out of hand. The horned
poppy biting the dust. – Looking
(always the patient, dogged
gaze) from north to east, a skyline
of spires and domes – curiously
devoid of human figures. Swift
gestural strokes,
like rampant, personal pronouns:
you and *I*, at a loss
for words, among dusty tinctures
of stubble.